Contents

GW00373998

 Published by: Arc International Cookware, Unit 3, Kingthorn Park, Bradden Road, Greens Norton, Towcester, NN12 8BS © 2008 Arc International Cookware ISBN: 9780956006004
E & OE

1

Hello and welcome to the National Baking Week book!

Now, before we start I just would like to get one thing straight. This may be a baking book, but it won't teach you how to bake a perfect cake – you certainly don't need another book to tell you that. No, what we hope to achieve from this book, and National Baking Week itself, is show what a good friend your oven is.

We attempt to make your oven a part of your daily life for both sweet and savoury recipes. There are many recipes that are perfect for when you can't be bothered at the end of a busy day and a few that will stretch you a little - designed for when you have a few hours to spare or guests to impress.

Baking can be such FUN! Baking Week is meant to inspire you. You can start now by trying one of these recipes, or by visiting www.nationalbakingweek.co.uk where you can see how else you can join us as we 'Get Britain Baking'.

Enjoy!   Rosemary Shrager

Hints and Equipment

OK, if you have never really baked before, getting started can be a little daunting - but it needn't be. A few simple tools – a mixing bowl, jug, a few baking trays, weighing scales, spatula and a wooden spoon are a good place to start.

Rule number one is look after your Pyrex bakeware and it will last for years - you don't need to scrub clean, Fairy dishwasher tablets or a little Fairy liquid are all you need. Once you become more confident, investing in other tools is a good idea. Kenwood mixers, which help to create an even consistency when beating, mixing and folding ingredients is a great next step – and they will last you a lifetime.

Now, the best advice to give when starting to bake is 'follow the recipe'. Sounds simple, but weights and measures can affect the outcome of the recipe quite considerably – so save the experimentation until you feel confident.

The recipes in this book are written in a way that is simple to understand and easy to follow. So read them through, make sure that you have everything you need prepared beforehand and let's get baking!

Bake 5

Quick after work dinners needn't be from a packet - and they needn't involve a huge list of ingredients. Our Bake 5 recipes are designed for simplicity and with 5 key ingredients, each will take 5 minutes to prepare. So what could be simpler? Stick them in the oven (with the timer on) and then get on with life. Do homework with the kids, get some chores out of the way or sit and read a magazine. Simply let your oven do the work!

Ingredients

100g Philadelphia Light with Garlic & Herbs
50g sliced white bread
Zest of 1 lemon
A few fresh chives, chopped
4 salmon fillets

Serves 4

Philadelphia Garlic & Herb Crusted Salmon

Pre-heat oven to 180°C/350°F/Gas Mark 4.

Place the bread in the mini bowl or multi mill of your Kenwood Food Processor and blend into fine breadcrumbs. Stir in the chives and lemon zest.

Spread the salmon fillets with a thick layer of Philly and place on a lightly oiled Pyrex Non-Stick Oven Tray. Top with the flavoured breadcrumbs, lightly pressing them into the Philly. Bake in the oven for 20-25 minutes or until cooked.

Equipment list

Pyrex Non-Stick Oven Tray
Kenwood Food Processor

Rosemary says

Salmon is high in Omega 3 that's reputed to have great health benefits.

Serve with salad leaves and new potatoes for a simple and tasty low fat dinner

Who ate all the pies?

Ingredients

375g packet of ready rolled shortcrust pastry
1 500g jar of readymade creamy mushroom sauce
1 small leek, finely sliced
100g cooked chicken, shredded
100g cooked ham, cut into cubes

Store Cupboard - Président Unsalted Butter, 1 British Lion egg

Serves 4

Individual Chicken, Leek & Ham Pies

Preheat the oven to 180°C/350°F/Gas Mark 4. Grease the Pyrex 4 Cup Pudding Tray.

Turn out the ready rolled pastry onto a floured surface and using a 12cm round cutter make 4 circles to form the base of each pie. Take a 10cm round cutter and cut a further 4 circles which will create the lids. Line the Pyrex 4 Cup Pudding Tray with the 12cm pastry circles ensuring a rim is left on each pie. Heat the readymade creamy mushroom sauce.

In a Pyrex Saucepan, sauté the sliced leeks over a medium heat with a knob of Président Butter until softened, taking approximately 5 minutes.

Add the sautéed leeks, the shredded chicken and the cooked ham to the heated sauce and season to taste. Generously spoon the filling into the Pyrex 4 Cup Pudding Tray so that the surface of the filling is slightly rounded.

Equipment list
Pyrex 4 Cup Pudding Tray
Pyrex Saucepan
10 & 12cm Round Pastry Cutters
Pastry Brush

Place the lids on top of the individual pies pressing the edges of the pastry together to seal the pies. Crimp the edges by pushing your thumb into the rim of the pastry and, using the thumb and forefinger of the other hand, gently pinch the pastry so that it is pushed up by this action. Continue around the edges of each individual pie.

Using the tip of a sharp knife make a few slits in the lid of each pie, so that the filling is visible, and glaze the pies with egg wash. Bake in the oven for 20 - 25 minutes until the pastry is golden.

Rosemary says

These will make a popular dinner, consider preparing a couple of batches and freezing some for another day.

British

Lion eggs

Ingredients
1 large British Lion egg
1 courgette, sliced
100g cherry tomatoes, halved
1tbsp snipped fresh basil leaves
15g low fat cheddar cheese, grated

Store Cupboard - 1tsp olive oil, Schwartz sea salt
& ground black pepper

Serves 1

Baked Eggs with Courgette & Tomatoes

Preheat the oven to 200°C/Fan 180°C/400°F/Gas Mark 6.

In a Pyrex Glass Ovenware Dish toss together the courgette, tomatoes, basil and oil with plenty of salt and freshly ground black pepper. Bake for 20 mins or until the courgette is pale golden.

Push the vegetables to the side of the dish to make a well in the centre; carefully crack the British Lion egg into the hole and sprinkle over the cheese. Bake for a further 8-10mins or until the egg is cooked to your liking. Serve hot with salad.

Equipment list
Pyrex Glass Ovenware Dish

Rosemary says

Use other vegetables, if you prefer, simply choose what is in season.

A quick and easy dinner for all the family

These smell great as they bake!

Ingredients

Président Slightly Salted Butter
6 portobello mushrooms
2 shallots, finely chopped
100g white breadcrumbs
250g stilton cheese, crumbled

Store Cupboard - Schwartz sea salt & freshly ground black pepper to season

Optional - 2tbsp Schwartz flat leaf parsley

Serves 6

Stilton Stuffed Mushrooms

Preheat the oven to 180°C/350°F/Gas Mark 4.

Remove the stalks from the portobello mushrooms, place the mushrooms onto a Pyrex Non-Stick Oven Tray and on a chopping board finely chop the mushroom stalks.

Place a knob of Président Slightly Salted Butter in a Pyrex Frying Pan – add the chopped shallots and mushroom stalks and sauté for approximately 5 minutes. Spoon the mixture evenly between the 6 flat mushrooms.

Mix the breadcrumbs, parsley (if using) and stilton cheese together. Generously spoon the breadcrumb mixture on top of each mushroom and season with salt and pepper.

Bake in the oven for 20-25 minutes until golden brown and cooked through.

Equipment list

Pyrex Non-Stick Oven Tray
Pyrex Frying Pan
Pyrex Mixing Bowl
Chopping Board

Rosemary says

A great dinner party starter - simply pop in the oven when guests arrive.

Ingredients

1tbsp Schwartz thyme
375g packet of ready rolled puff pastry
1 red onion, finely sliced
100g cherry tomatoes, sliced in half
200g soft rinded goats' cheese, divided into bite-sized pieces

Store Cupboard - Président Unsalted Butter, 1 British Lion egg yolk

Serves 4

Goats' Cheese, Tomato & Onion Tarts

Preheat the oven to 180°C/ 350°F/Gas Mark 4.

Take the puff pastry and using a 12cm round cutter make 4 round circles to form the base of each tart. Prick each base with a fork and place onto a Pyrex Non-Stick Oven Tray.

Place a knob of butter in a Pyrex Frying Pan over a medium heat, add the sliced onion and sauté until softened, for approximately 5 minutes. Leave to cool.

Assemble the tarts: leaving a slight edge (approx 1cm), evenly spoon the sautéed onion, cherry tomatoes and pieces of goats' cheese onto each base, sprinkle with Schwartz thyme and season.

Finally, glaze the tarts by brushing egg yolk around the rim. Place in the oven and cook for 15 minutes or until golden brown.

Equipment list
Pyrex Non-Stick Oven Tray
Pyrex Frying Pan
12cm Round Pastry Cutter
Pastry Brush

Rosemary says

Baking tomatoes gives them a sticky sweetness – it works perfectly with salty goats' cheese.

Simply dress with a little rocket or watercress then serve

Great to bake with the kids!

Ingredients
175g Lyle's Golden Syrup
100g Président Unsalted Butter
1 British Lion egg
175g wholemeal self raising flour
150g chopped almonds

Store Cupboard - 50g caster sugar

Makes 36

Nutty Golden Syrup Cookies

Preheat the oven to 160°C/300°F/Gas Mark 2.

Grease 3 Pyrex Non-Stick Oven Trays.

Cream the butter, sugar and Lyle's Golden Syrup together until light and fluffy. Beat in the egg.

Sift the flour and lightly beat into the mixture then fold in chopped almonds.

Place small spoonfuls of the mixture onto the oven trays, allowing plenty of room for them to spread (6 spoonfuls per tray).

Bake in the oven for 9 minutes or until golden brown. Allow to firm slightly before transferring onto a wire rack.

Repeat the last 2 steps with the remaining mixture.

Equipment list
Pyrex Mixing Bowl
3 x Pyrex Non-Stick Oven Trays
Sieve

Rosemary says

Bake in batches and store in an airtight container for later – if they last that long.

Ingredients
90g Président Unsalted Butter, (plus extra for greasing)
2 whole British Lion eggs and 2 British Lion egg yolks
40g wholemeal plain flour
40g caster sugar, plus extra for dusting
100g dark chocolate (70% minimum cocoa solids)

Serves 4

Melting Chocolate Fondants

Preheat the oven to 180°C/350°F/Gas Mark 4.

Heavily grease 4 x 9cm Pyrex Ceramic Ramekins with Président Unsalted Butter and dust the inside with caster sugar, gently tapping out any excess.

Beat the whole eggs and egg yolks with the caster sugar, in a Kenwood Chef using the ballon whisk, until light and fluffy, taking approximately 8-10 minutes.

Melt the chocolate and Président Unsalted Butter together in a bain-marie, over a pan of simmering water, being careful not to let the chocolate get too hot as it will burn and taint the flavour.

When the egg mixture is sufficiently aerated gently fold in the flour. Take a small amount of egg mixture and beat it into the melted chocolate, then carefully fold the chocolate mixture to the remaining egg mixture.

Fill each Pyrex Ceramic Ramekin with the fondant mixture and bake in the oven for 11 minutes. Serve immediately, dusted with cocoa powder if desired.

Equipment list
4 x 9cm Pyrex Ceramic Ramekins
Bain-Marie (Pyrex Mixing Bowl over pan of simmering water)
Pyrex Saucepan
Kenwood Chef
Sieve

Rosemary says

The egg mixture should stand in peaks after whisking or your fondants won't rise.

Perfect way to finish a romantic dinner for two

Perfect for when you have unexpected guests

Ingredients

150g Philadelphia Light
4 ripe peaches, cut in half and stone removed
25g caster sugar
50g amaretto biscuits, crushed
75g fresh raspberries, cut in half

Serves 4

Philadelphia Baked Peaches

Preheat the oven to 190°C/375°F/Gas Mark 5.

Place the peach halves into a Pyrex Glass Oval Roaster. Mix together the Philly and caster sugar until well blended. Top each of the peaches with generous spoonfuls of the Philly mixture.

Sprinkle the peaches with the crushed amaretto biscuits and raspberries. Cover with foil and bake in the oven for 10 minutes. Remove the foil and bake for a further 10 minutes. Serve warm.

Equipment list
Pyrex Glass Oval Roaster
Pyrex Mixing Bowl

Rosemary says

This dessert is so delicious! You can put it together in minutes, but it looks really impressive.

British
Lion eggs

Ingredients
2 large British Lion eggs
1 small brioche loaf
250g blackberries
285ml milk
25g flaked almonds

Store Cupboard - 25g caster sugar

Serves 4

Blackberry & Almond Bread & Butter Pudding

Preheat the oven to 180°C/350°F/Gas Mark 4.

Slice the brioche loaf and then cut into triangles. Layer the slices into a 20cm Pyrex Non-Stick Cake Pan.

Beat together the 2 British Lion eggs, milk and sugar. Pour half the egg mixture over the brioche, allow approximately 5 minutes for the brioche to absorb the mixture before adding the remaining liquid.

Arrange the blackberries over the soaked brioche and bake in the oven for 15 minutes. Sprinkle the almonds over the bread and butter pudding and cook for a further 10 minutes.

Equipment list
20cm Pyrex Non-Stick Cake Pan
Pyrex Mixing Bowl

Rosemary says
Freeze blackberries when they are in season and you can make this throughout the winter.

Lovely served hot with Greek yoghurt

Ideal for parties, these simply melt in the mouth!

Ingredients
375g packet of ready rolled puff pastry
200g Philadelphia
30g caster sugar
2tbsp redcurrant jelly
450g strawberries, hulled and sliced in half

Store Cupboard - 1 British Lion egg

Serves 8

Open Individual Strawberry Tarts

Preheat the oven to 180°C/350°F/Gas Mark 4.

Turn out the ready rolled puff pastry and make 8 heart bases using a 10cm heart-shaped cutter. Place the tart bases onto a greased Pyrex Non-Stick Oven Tray and with the tip of a sharp knife make a shallow heart-shaped cut about 8mm from the edge to form a picture frame style border.

Brush the pastry edges with beaten egg to glaze and bake in the oven for about 15 minutes until well risen. Take the tarts out of the oven and scoop out the risen centres of the pastries. Leave to cool.

Beat the Philly with the sugar until smooth, pile the mixture into the centre of the cooled pastry cases and level off.

Melt the redcurrant jelly over a medium heat to make the glaze. Arrange the strawberry halves over the Philly mixture and brush lightly with the glaze.

Equipment list
Pyrex Non-Stick Oven Tray
Pyrex Mixing Bowl
Pyrex Saucepan
10cm Heart Shaped Cutter
Pastry Brush

Rosemary says

The more you beat the Philly mixture the lighter it will be.

Ingredients

2 large pork chump chops, trimmed of fat
Schwartz sea salt & freshly ground black
pepper to season
45ml (3tbsp) Lyle's Golden Syrup
30ml (2tbsp) soy sauce
45ml (3tbsp) tomato purée
1tsp of Schwartz garlic granules
2.5ml (½tsp) mustard powder
Juice of 1 large orange
Juice of 1 lemon
15ml (1tbsp) white wine vinegar
15ml (1tbsp) vegetable oil
1 small onion, peeled & chopped
1 red pepper, deseeded and sliced

Serves 2

Equipment list

Pyrex Mixing Bowl
Pyrex Frying Pan
Pyrex Ceramic Gratin Dish

Barbecued Pork Chops

Preheat the oven to 180°C/350°F/Gas Mark 4.

Season the chops well. In a Pyrex Mixing Bowl
mix together the golden syrup, soy sauce,
tomato purée, garlic, mustard, fruit juices
and vinegar.

Heat the oil in a Pyrex Frying Pan and fry the
chops quickly on both sides until browned.
Remove the chops from the pan and place
them into a Pyrex Ceramic Gratin Dish.

In the same pan, sauté the chopped onion
together with the red pepper for
approximately 5 minutes until softened.

Pour the sauce mixture over the chops and
scatter over the sautéed onion and peppers.
Cover, and cook in the oven for 30-40 minutes
until tender. Serve with rice if desired.

Ingredients

400g Allinson Very Strong Wholemeal Flour
250g Allinson Very Strong White Flour
7g sachet Allinson Easy Bake Yeast
100g walnut pieces, chopped and toasted
2tbsp unrefined light muscovado sugar
1½tsp Schwartz sea salt
3tbsp walnut, sunflower or olive oil
450ml warm water

Makes 1 loaf

Equipment list

Pyrex Mixing Bowl
Pyrex Non-Stick Oven Tray

Chunky Walnut Bread

Put the Allinson Very Strong Wholemeal Flour
into a large Pyrex Mixing Bowl with the
Allinson Very Strong White Flour. Add the
walnut pieces, muscovado sugar and salt.

Sprinkle over the Allinson Easy Bake yeast.
Pour in the oil and warm water.

Mix together with your hands until the mixture
combines to make a rough dough ball.

Tip the dough out onto a lightly floured
surface and stretch and knead the dough
for 10 minutes until smooth and elastic.

Shape into an oval and put on to a greased
Pyrex Non-Stick Oven Tray. Use a sharp knife
to score a few diagonal lines on top
of the loaf. Cover loosely with cling film.
Leave in a warm place until doubled in size
(This will take about 30-40 minutes).

Preheat the oven to 220°C/200°C Fan/Gas
Mark 7.

Remove cling film from bread and reduce
the oven temperature to 200°C/180°C
Fan/Gas Mark 6. Bake the bread for
35 minutes until golden.

To test to see if the loaf is ready, upturn and
tap the base - it should sound hollow.

Breadmaker method

Adjust the above ingredients in the
following way;

350g Allinson Very Strong Wholemeal Flour
150g Allinson Very Strong White Flour
1tsp Allinson Easy Bake Yeast
350ml warm water
All other ingredients as before

Put all the ingredients into the bread maker
bucket following the order and method
specified in the manual.

Fit the bucket into the bread maker and set
to the basic programme with a light crust.
Press start.

Ingredients

225g whole medjool dates, stoned and finely chopped
175g boiling water
85g Président Unsalted Butter, softened, plus extra for greasing
140g demerara sugar
2 British Lion eggs, beaten
2tbsp Lyle's Black Treacle
1tsp vanilla extract
175g wholemeal self raising flour, plus extra for greasing
1tsp bicarbonate of soda
100ml milk

Toffee Sauce:
175g light muscovado sugar
50g Président Butter, cut into pieces
225ml double cream
1tbsp Lyle's Black Treacle

Serves 4

Sticky Toffee Pudding

Preheat the oven to 180°C/350°F/Gas Mark 4. Grease 4 Pyrex Individual Oval Pie Dishes.

Put the dates into a bowl, add the boiling water and leave for 30 minutes until cooled and well-soaked. Mash the dates with a fork to make a pulp.

Meanwhile beat the butter and sugar together in a large bowl until slightly creamy. Add the eggs a little at a time, beating well after each addition then mix in the black treacle and vanilla extract.

Mix the flour and bicarbonate of soda together. Gently fold the one-third of the flour and half the milk into the pudding batter, being careful not to overbeat. Repeat until all the flour and milk has been used, and then stir in the date pulp to the mixture.

Spoon the batter into the Pyrex Individual Oval Pie Dishes and bake for 20-25 minutes, until risen and firm.

Next make the toffee sauce: put the sugar and butter in a Pyrex Saucepan with half the cream. Bring to the boil over a medium heat, stirring all the time, until the sugar has completely dissolved. Stir in the black treacle, turn up the heat slightly and let the mixture bubble away for 2-3 minutes until it is a rich toffee colour, stirring occasionally to make sure it doesn't burn. Take the pan off the heat and beat in the rest of the cream.

Remove the puddings from the oven, and serve warm with a drizzling of sauce.

Equipment list
Pyrex Mixing Bowls
4 Pyrex Individual Oval Pie Dishes
Pyrex Saucepan

Ingredients

150g Alllinson Wholemeal Self Raising Flour
75g golden caster sugar
½tsp Schwartz sea salt
75g pecan nuts, chopped
Zest of 1 orange finely grated
1 British Lion egg
2tbsp orange juice
100ml milk
75g Président Unsalted Butter, melted

Makes 12

Easy Orange & Pecan Muffins

Preheat the oven to 180°C/160°C Fan/Gas Mark 4. Put the golden caster sugar, Allinson Wholemeal Self Raising Flour, salt, pecan nuts and orange zest into a bowl.

In a Pyrex Jug mix together the egg, orange juice, milk and melted butter.

Pour the wet ingredients into the dry and gently mix together.

Line a Pyrex Non-Stick Muffin Tray with 12 paper muffin cases. Spoon the mixture into the cases. Bake for 15 minutes until risen.

Tip: Instead of muffins, pour this mixture into a greased and lined 900g/2lb loaf tin and bake for 40 minutes until a skewer inserted into the centre comes out clean.

Equipment list

Pyrex Jug
Pyrex Non-Stick Muffin Tray

Pyrex Mixing Bowl
Muffin Cases
Sieve

Ingredients

2tsp Schwartz flat leaf parsley
250g double cream
100ml milk
1tbsp wholegrain mustard
250g fresh spinach, wilted and well drained
200g cooked shelled prawns
200g skinned, un-dyed, smoked haddock, cut
into large chunks
200g skinned salmon fillet, cut into large chunks
50g breadcrumbs
Rind of a lemon

Serves 6

Creamy Seafood & Spinach Bake

Preheat the oven to 180°C/350°F/Gas Mark 4.

Mix together the double cream, milk and wholegrain mustard. Place the wilted spinach in the base of a Pyrex Ceramic Rectangular Roaster, add the prawns, haddock and salmon. Pour over the cream mixture, season and bake in the oven for 10 minutes.

Meanwhile mix together the breadcrumbs, parsley and lemon rind, scatter over the top of the bake and put in the oven for a further 15 minutes until the topping is golden brown.

Serve with chunks of crusty bread.

Equipment list

Pyrex Ceramic Rectangular Roaster
Pyrex Mixing Bowl

Ingredients

200g Philadelphia
2tbsp fresh chives, chopped
2 garlic cloves, crushed
1 onion, peeled and finely chopped
Schwartz sea salt & freshly ground
black pepper to season
4 chicken breasts
12-16 rashes of streaky, smoked
bacon
Lyle's Golden Syrup pouring bottle

Serves 4

Savoury Chicken Parcels Wrapped in Bacon

Preheat the oven to 200°C/400°F/Gas Mark 6.

In a bowl mix together the Philly, chives, garlic, onion and seasoning to make the filling.

Slice three-quarters of the way horizontally through each of the chicken breasts, open out and divide the filling between each of the breasts. Fold the chicken back over, then form a parcel. Wrap each of the parcels with 3-4 slices of bacon, starting at the thin end and wrapping round and round to secure the chicken inside. Secure with a couple of cocktail sticks.

Place the chicken parcels onto a Pyrex Non-Stick Oven Tray, drizzle each with a little pouring golden syrup and cook in the oven for about 30-35 minutes or until crisp and cooked through.

Serve with a crisp salad if desired.

Equipment list

Pyrex Mixing Bowl
Pyrex Non-Stick Oven Tray
Chopping Board
Cocktail Sticks

Ingredients

510g Lyle's Golden Syrup
115g desiccated coconut
200ml double cream
1 British Lion egg white, lightly beaten
Granulated sugar for dusting

For the pastry:
150g Président Unsalted Butter
340g wholemeal plain flour
1 large British Lion egg yolk
40ml water

Serves 10

Coconut Syrup Tart

Preheat the oven to 180°C/350°F/Gas Mark 4. Lightly grease a Pyrex Non-Stick 30cm Flan Pan.

First make the pastry. Rub the butter into the flour until the mixture resembles fine breadcrumbs. Beat the egg yolk with the water and stir into the flour mixture to make a dough.

Roll out two thirds of the dough and use to line the Pyrex Flan Pan.

To make the filling, mix the Lyle's Golden Syrup with the desiccated coconut and double cream. Spread evenly over the base of the pastry case.

Roll out the remaining pastry, cut into thin strips and arrange them in a lattice pattern on top of the flan. Bake in the oven for 20 minutes.

Carefully brush the lattice strips with lightly beaten egg white, and sprinkle with sugar. Return the flan to the oven for a further 15-20 minutes until golden brown. Serve warm with cream if desired.

Equipment list

Pyrex Non-Stick 30cm Flan Pan
Pyrex Mixing Bowl
Pyrex Jug
Pastry Brush
Rolling Pin

Ingredients

1tsp Schwartz ground nutmeg
1tsp Schwartz ground cinnamon
250g pumpkin flesh, cooked until tender, then puréed
60g chopped walnuts
225g strong flour
225g dark brown sugar

70g caster sugar
¾tsp of bicarbonate soda
½tsp Schwartz sea salt
100g Unsalted Président Butter, melted
75ml coconut milk
50g flaked coconut

Makes 1 loaf

Spiced Pumpkin Tea Bread

Preheat oven to 350°F/175°C/Gas Mark 4.

Spread walnuts in a single layer on a Pyrex Non-Stick Oven Tray. Toast in the preheated oven for 8 to 10 minutes, or until lightly browned. Set aside to cool.

In a large Pyrex Mixing Bowl, stir together the flour, brown sugar, caster sugar, baking soda, Schwartz sea salt, Schwartz ground nutmeg and Schwartz ground cinnamon.

Add the pumpkin purée, butter, and coconut milk, and mix until all of the flour is absorbed. Fold in the flaked coconut and toasted walnuts. Turn into the Pyrex Loaf Pan.

Bake for 1 hour and 15 minutes in the preheated oven, or until a skewer inserted in the centre comes out clean.

Equipment list
Pyrex Non-Stick Baking Tray
Pyrex Mixing Bowl
Pyrex Loaf Pan

Ingredients

1kilo pumpkin, deseeded
25g Président Unsalted Butter
2 large onions, peeled and sliced
2 garlic cloves, peeled and chopped
1 red chilli, deseeded & chopped
750ml vegetable stock
1tsp Schwartz ground cumin
375ml whole milk
Schwartz sea salt & freshly ground
black pepper to season

For the goats' cheese croutons:
1 small baguette, cut into slices
2 tbsps olive oil
125g English soft goats' cheese

Serves 6

Spiced Roasted Pumpkin Soup with Goats' Cheese Croutons

Preheat the oven to 200°C/400°F/Gas Mark 6.

Place the pieces of pumpkin flesh-side down on a large Pyrex Non-Stick Baking Tray. Cover tightly with foil and cook in the oven for 1 hour. Remove from the oven and scoop out all the flesh and set aside.

Roast the pumpkin. Melt the butter in a Pyrex Saucepan and sauté the onions, garlic and red chilli until soft but not brown.

Add the cooked pumpkin flesh, stock, cumin and seasoning. Bring to the boil and simmer for 15 minutes.

While the soup is cooking, make the croutons:

Brush the bread slices with olive oil, place on a Pyrex Non-Stick Oven Tray and bake in the oven until crispy and golden. This will take 5-10 minutes.

When the soup is cooked and cooled slightly, blend in the glass liquidiser attachment of your Kenwood Food Processor.

Return to a clean pan and add the milk. Reheat the soup without allowing it to boil. Check the seasoning.

Spread the cooked croutons with the soft goats' cheese.

Serve the cooked soup in warm bowls with the croutons on the side, or even placed on top just before serving.

Equipment list

Pyrex Non-Stick Oven Tray
Pyrex Saucepan
Pyrex Frying Pan

Chopping Board
Kenwood Food Processor

Ingredients

450g piece of pumpkin
1tbsp olive oil
Pinch of Schwartz fennel seeds, crushed
1 British Lion egg yolk
25g parmesan cheese, grated
Pinch of Schwartz ground nutmeg
15g fresh white breadcrumbs
Schwartz sea salt & freshly ground black
pepper to season

Fresh Egg Pasta:
400g "00" flour
Pinch of salt
3 whole British Lion eggs
2 British Lion egg yolks

Sage Butter:
75g Président Unsalted Butter
20 small sage leaves
Extra grated parmesan cheese to serve

Serves 4

Pumpkin Ravioli in a Butter & Sage Sauce

Preheat the oven to 200°C/400°F/Gas Mark 6.

Cut the pumpkin in half, scoop out the seeds and cut into large chunks. Put onto a Pyrex Non-Stick Oven Tray, add the oil, sprinkle with fennel seeds and season.

Roast until the pumpkin is tender, taking approximately 30 minutes. Leave to cool slightly before scooping the flesh away from the skin.

Put the pumpkin flesh in a Pyrex Mixing Bowl and mash until smooth. Mix in the egg yolk, parmesan, nutmeg, breadcrumbs and season to taste.

For the pasta dough:
Mix the flour and salt together and place on a work surface, and make a well in the centre. Place the eggs in the middle and start to work the flour into the egg mix until it comes together into a ball. Knead the pasta dough slightly until it become silky to touch.

Roll out the pasta using a pasta machine, lightly dusting the dough with flour between rolls.

To make the ravioli place the piece of dough on a floured surface and make small indentations over the bottom half of it at 6cm intervals. Place a teaspoon of the pumpkin filling on each mark and then brush lines of egg wash between them.

Fold over the top half of the dough and working from the centre of the line outwards press firmly around the filling to push out any trapped air and seal in the filling. Trim off the edges and then cut between the rows with a fluted pasta wheel.

Cook the ravioli in boiling, salted water for 3-4 minutes.

For the sage butter, melt the butter in a Pyrex Frying Pan until foaming, throw in the sage and fry for a few seconds.

Put the ravioli into a serving bowl, pour over the sage butter, season and sprinkle with parmesan cheese if desired. Serve immediately.

Equipment list

Pasta Machine
Pasta Wheel
Pyrex Non-Stick Oven Tray

Pyrex Mixing Bowl
Pyrex Saucepan
Pyrex Frying Pan

The BEST EVER degreasing power*

from FAIRY

FOR DISHWASHERS

POWERSPRAY ACTION

Recommended by

Pyrex is a trademark of Corning Inc., used by permission

FAIRY
ACTIVE BURSTS
LEMON

WITH THE CLEANING POWER OF FAIRY

9 911194 371009 >

* within the Fairy Dishwasher range

THE KENWOOD CHEF
– ready to help you in your quest for healthy, nutritious food

Create perfect dinner party recipes, treats for your family and special dishes for your friends simply and easily with your Chef.

KENWOOD

HONEST HOME MADE GOODNESS!

There are many reasons why it seems appropriate now to be thinking about what's in our diets and how our food is made. As we eat more healthily we are keen to know what exactly we are eating and where it has come from.

Dr Thomas Allinson, the founder of Allinson Flour, was a firm believer in such things over 100 years ago. Despite being 'struck off' as a doctor because of his revolutionary views, Allinson persisted in his belief that healthy eating was the basis of a healthy lifestyle – and to prove the point he created the wholemeal flour that continues to bear his name.

Over the intervening years we have developed a range of high quality flours, but have always been true to the no nonsense approach of our founder. And now at Allinson, we find ourselves back in fashion. The taste, texture and quality of home made bread and baking appeal to people more than ever before. Baking it yourself makes sense. No nasty this and that, just good, honest, wholesome ingredients for you and your family.

And that's why we've launched **www.bakingmad.com**. This website is crammed full of hints, tips and inspirational recipes all designed to inspire you and your family to get back to baking! There's also the opportunity to join the baking club and receive e-newsletters, exclusive competitions and product offers!

Allinson Country Grain Bread

Makes 1 large loaf
650g (1lb 7oz) Allinson Country Grain Strong Bread Flour
1tsp salt
1tsp Billington's Unrefined Light Muscovado sugar
25g (1oz) butter, chopped
7g sachet Allinson Easy Bake Yeast
450ml (³/₄pt) warm water

1. Put the Country Grain Strong Bread Flour into a large bowl. Add the salt, Muscovado sugar and butter and rub into the flour to combine.

2. Sprinkle over the Easy Bake Yeast. Pour in the warm water.

3. Mix together with your hands until the mixture combines to make a rough dough ball.

4. Tip the dough out onto a lightly floured surface and stretch and knead the dough for 10 minutes until smooth and elastic.

5. Shape into a round and place on a greased baking tray. Use a sharp knife to score a cross in the centre of the loaf. Cover loosely with cling film. Leave in a warm place until doubled in size. (This will take about 30-40 minutes.)

6. Preheat the oven to 220°C/fan 200°C/gas 7. Remove cling film from bread and reduce the oven temperature to 200°C/fan 180°C/gas 6. Bake the bread for 35 minutes until golden. To test to see if the loaf is ready, upturn and tap the base – it should sound hollow.

TIP: *Why not add 2tbsp of sunflower or poppy seeds in step one to add extra flavour and texture?*

Breadmaker method
Adjust the above ingredients in the following way;
Use 500g (1lb 2oz) Allinson Country Grain Strong Bread Flour
1tsp Allinson Easy Bake Yeast
350ml (12floz) warm water

• Put all the ingredients into the bread maker following the method specified in the manual.

Allinson Flour

*Pure butter made in
the heart of Normandy*

Président® makes everyday occasions taste more special

Golden Flapjack

75g (3oz) butter
100g (4oz) Tate & Lyle
Light Brown Soft Sugar
60ml (2 rounded tbsp)
Lyle's Golden Syrup
175g (6oz) rolled oats
Makes 8 fingers

Grease a 20cm (8 inch) square baking tin and preheat the oven to 180 degrees C, 350 degrees F, gas mark 4.

Heat the butter, sugar and syrup in a saucepan until the butter has melted, stir in the rolled oats. Press the mixture into the tin and bake in the oven for about 20 minutes.

Cut into fingers whilst still warm, then leave to finish cooling in the tin before turning out.

Two deliciously simple recipes from Lyle's

Lyle's Black Treacle Toffee

450g (1lb) Tate & Lyle
Granulated Sugar
150ml (1/4 pt) water
1/4 tsp cream of tartar
75g (3oz) butter or margarine
100g (4oz) Lyle's Black Treacle
100g (4oz) Lyle's Golden Syrup
Makes 8 fingers

Boil to the soft crack stage or 132 -14 degrees C, 270 - 290 degrees F. The best way to do this is to use a sugar thermometer. Alternatively, drop a little of the mixture into a bowl of cold water and if the syrup separates into threads which are hard, but not brittle, it is ready.

Lightly oil an 18cm (7 inch) shallow square tin. Measure the sugar and water into a large heavy-based non-stick saucepan and heat gently until the sugar has dissolved. Add the cream of tartar, butter, treacle and syrup and bring to the boil. Brush the inside of the pan with water, just above the level of the sugar syrup.

Pour into the tin, cool for 5 minutes then mark into squares with an oile knife and leave to set in a cool plac (not the refrigerator).